MONSTER

PHONICS

Consonant Blends
& Digraphs

For Grades 1–2

By Vicky Shiotsu

Illustrated by Lucy Helle

LOWELL HOUSE JUVENILE

LOS ANGELES

NTC/Contemporary Publishing Group

Reviewed and endorsed by Judith Ozeran-Hansen,
Certified Language Development Specialist, Veteran Elementary
Teacher, and Former Lead Teacher at Sylvan Learning Center

About the Author

Vicky Shiotsu graduated from the University of British Columbia with a Bachelor's degree in Education and taught elementary school at various grade levels for eight years. She has also worked as a tutor to Japanese students, a teacher at a reading center, and as an editor/writer for an educational publishing company.

Published by Lowell House
A division of NTC/Contemporary Publishing Group, Inc.
4255 West Touhy Avenue, Lincolnwood (Chicago), Illinois 60646-1975 U.S.A.

Managing Director and Publisher: Jack Artenstein
Director of Publishing Services: Rena Copperman
Editorial Director: Brenda Pope-Ostrow
Director of Art Production: Bret Perry
Editor: Linda Gorman
Designer: Carolyn Wendt
Color Artist: Kristi Mathias

Series logo created by Jack Keely

Lowell House books can be purchased at special discounts when ordered in bulk for premiums and special sales. Please contact Customer Service at:
NTC/Contemporary Publishing Group
4255 West Touhy Avenue
Lincolnwood, IL 60646-1975
1-800-323-4900

Printed in Hong Kong by Imago

ISBN: 0-7373-0220-8

10 9 8 7 6 5 4 3 2 1

Note to Parents

Monster Phonics is a wonderful learning tool that will help your child build a strong foundation in phonics. A community of lovable monsters present and teach the activities in this workbook, helping your child develop a knowledge of consonant blends (consonants that combine to produce a "blended" sound, such as the *cr* in *crayon*) and consonant digraphs (consonants that produce a single sound, such as the *sh* in *ship*). The appealing activities also encourage listening and reading comprehension, analytical thinking, and problem solving. What a great way to instill a love of learning!

The activities in this book offer your child opportunities to practice a wide range of skills. Activities include distinguishing letter sounds, reading and writing words, solving riddles, completing puzzles, and more! It is best that your child complete the activities in the order that they are presented, since some of the pages build on skills practiced earlier in the book.

As your child works through the pages, give plenty of praise and encouragement. Each activity is designed to ensure success and stimulate interest. If your child likes to work independently, let him or her do so. If your child prefers to read the sentences with you, then by all means do that. After each activity is done, you and your child can turn to the back of the book to check the answers. Later, when all the pages have been completed, present your child with the colorful award provided on the last page of the book.

Learning is an exciting and rewarding experience. Whether your child is a phonics marvel or is just becoming aware of the relationship between letters and sounds, he or she will benefit from each motivating activity in the **Monster Phonics** series! You will find that as your child masters the various skills presented in these activity books, he or she will develop and display the traits of a confident, enthusiastic learner.

BLENDS AND DIGRAPHS CHART

Say the name of each picture. Listen to the beginning sound.

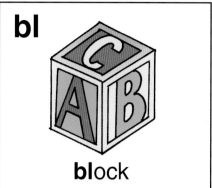

bl

block

br

brick

cl

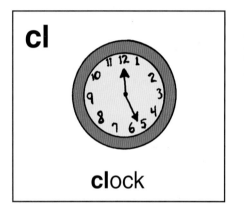

clock

cr

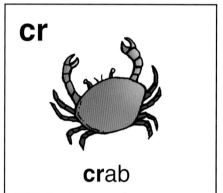

crab

dr

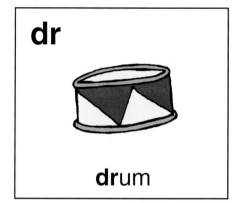

drum

fl

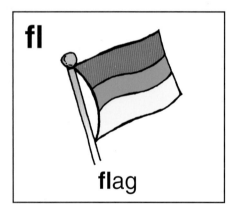

flag

fr

frog

gl

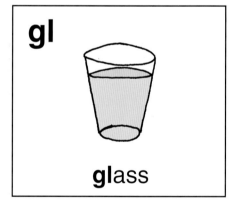

glass

gr

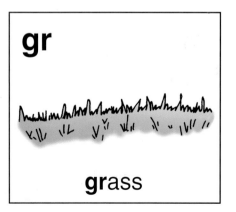

grass

pl

plant

pr

prize

4

Introduction to consonant blends and digraphs

sk

skunk

sl

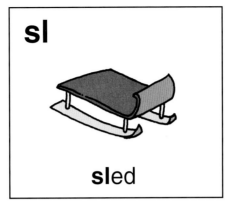

sled

sm

smoke

sn

snake

sp

spider

st

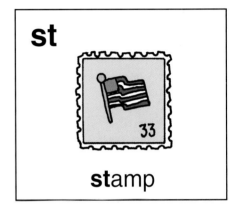

stamp

sw

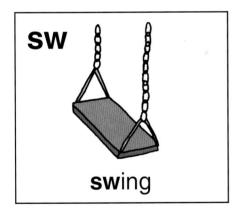

swing

tr

tree

ch

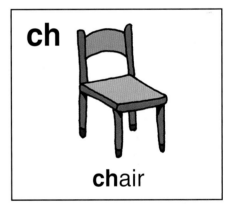

chair

sh

sheep

th

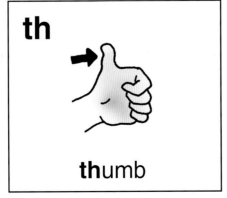

thumb

wh

whale

Introduction to consonant blends and digraphs

HELP BLIP

Help Blip with his homework. Read the sentences below. Circle the words that begin with **bl** and write them on the lines. Then color the pictures.

1. Color the blimp red.

_____

2. Color the bluebird blue.

_____

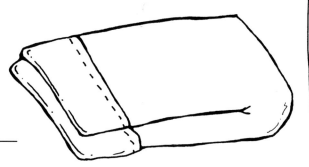

3. Color the blanket yellow.

_____

4. Color the toy block green.

_____

6

*Reading words that begin with **bl***

CLEO'S CLUES

Read Cleo's clues below. Write the **cl** word that matches each clue. Use the words in the box.

clam	clock	claws	club	clay

1. This helps you tell the time. _____

2. This animal has a shell. _____

3. A cat has these on its feet. _____

4. You can make a pot out of this. _____

5. This is a big stick. _____

Use the words in the box to label the pictures.

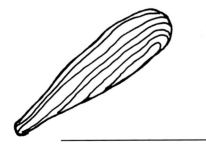 _____

 _____

 _____

_____

 _____

FLORA'S CHALLENGE

Flora wrote **flashlight** to make a word puzzle. Look at the picture clues. Use the **fl** words in the box to complete the puzzle.

flag	fly	flame	flower	flute

Clues

1.

2.

3.

4.

5.

GLIB AND GLUB

The sentences below tell about Glib and Glub. Write the correct **gl** word to complete each sentence.

1. Glib looks _____, but Glub looks sad.
   glad, glum

2. Glib has a _____ in her hand.
   glee, glass

3. Glub is holding some _____.
   glue, gleam

4. Glub has a hand on a _____.
   globe, glide

5. Glub has _____ that help him see.
   glaze, glasses

Why do you think Glub looks glum?

_____

_____

Reading words that begin with gl   **9**

VISIT THE PLANETS

Help the monsters visit the planets. Look at the picture on each planet. Write its name. Use the **pl** words on the spaceship.

plum   plate   plant
plug   plane   plank

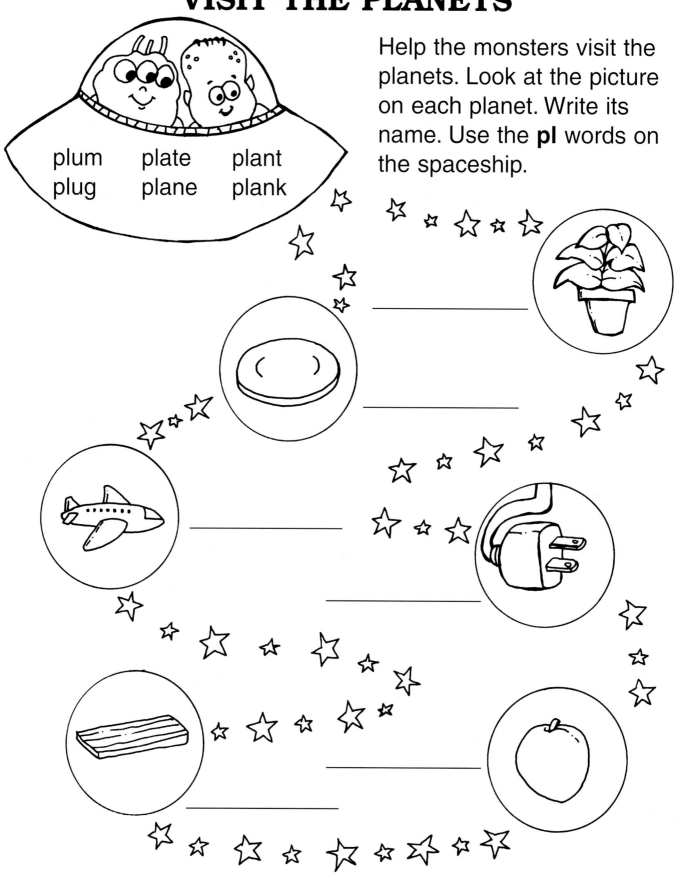

Reading words that begin with pl

SLEEP AND DREAM

Complete the sentences to tell about the picture. Use the **sl** words in the box.

slug	slick	sliding	sleeping	sled	slippers

1. Slimy is _____ in bed.

2. Her _____ are under the bed.

3. Her toy _____ is on the blanket.

4. Slimy is dreaming of a new _____.

5. In her dream, she is _____ down a hill.

6. The hill is very _____!

Reading words that begin with sl   **11**

IN THE CLOUDS

Look at the pictures in the clouds. Say their names. Write the missing blend for each word.

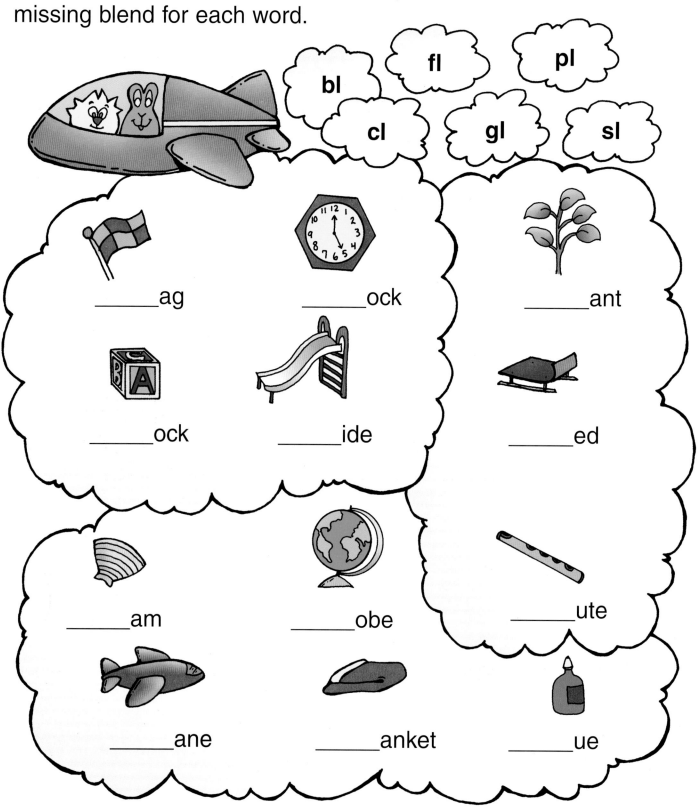

bl   fl   pl   cl   gl   sl

_____ag

_____ock

_____ant

_____ock

_____ide

_____ed

_____am

_____obe

_____ute

_____ane

_____anket

_____ue

Review of l blends

LET'S PLAY

Write the correct word to complete each sentence.

1. Let's play with some _____.
   blot, blocks

2. Let's make a _____ pot.
   clay, clap

3. Let's wave a blue _____.
   flag, flat

4. Let's look at a _____.
   glide, globe

5. Let's fly a toy _____.
   plane, plant

6. Let's go down the _____.
   slide, slap

7. Let's get some paper and _____.
   glum, glue

8. Let's ride the _____ down the hill.
   sled, slim

BRUNO'S WORDS

Bruno made a list of **br** words. Read the words. Then use them to label the pictures.

brick

bride

braid

branch

brush

bracelet

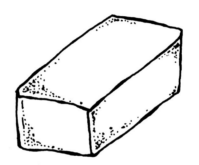

_____

_____

_____

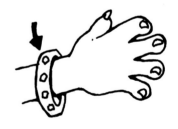

_____

_____

_____

*Reading words that begin with **br***

CRUSTY'S CROWNS

Crusty made paper crowns. Write **cr** on the lines to finish the words on the crowns.

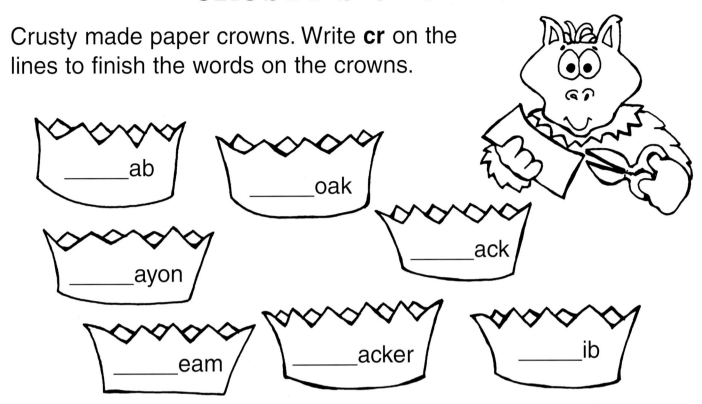

_____ab

_____oak

_____ack

_____ayon

_____eam

_____acker

_____ib

Use the words on the crowns to complete the sentences.

1. A _____ lives by the sea.

2. The baby is asleep in the _____.

3. I will put some jam on this _____.

4. A toad can _____.

5. You may use my blue _____ to color.

6. The cup got a _____ when I dropped it.

7. Mom put some _____ in her coffee.

DRU'S DRAWINGS

Look at Dru's drawings. The name of each picture begins with **dr**. Add **dr** to the words in the box. Then use the words to label the drawings.

_____um	_____ess	_____agon
_____ape	_____ill	_____esser

  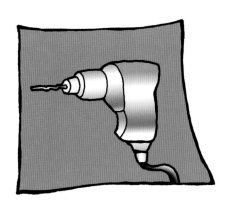

_____ _____ _____

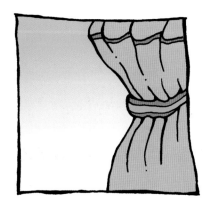  

_____ _____ _____

Reading words that begin with dr

FRIENDLY FROGS

Read the **fr** words on the frogs.
Use the words to complete the
sentences below.

1. A _____ can hop fast.

2. Frank picked some _____ to eat.

3. I will _____ an egg for lunch.

4. This picture has a green _____ around it.

5. We got _____ tickets, so we did not have to pay.

6. When it is cold, there is _____ on the windows.

7. We will buy _____ fish at the market.

A GREAT SNACK

green

grass

grape

grin

grand

Complete the sentences. Use the **gr** words in the box.

1. Greta sits on the _____.

2. A big _____ frog sits by Greta.

3. Greta has a big _____ on her face.

4. She gets some crackers and _____ jelly.

5. Greta and the frog have a _____ time snacking!

Draw a picture of
what you think is
a great snack.
Label your picture.

*Reading words that begin with **gr***

PRETTY PRESENTS

Read the **pr** words on the presents.

Use the **pr** words to complete the sentences.

1. I can _____ my name.

2. Anna won the first _____ in the contest.

3. What is the _____ of that toy?

4. Do not _____ yourself with that pin.

5. Matt played a _____ on his sister.

6. The roses are very _____.

7. We worked on a math _____ together.

A TRUCKLOAD OF WORDS

Help the driver get to the end of the road. Add **tr** to the words on the truck. Then use the words to label the pictures on the road.

_____uck _____ee

_____ay _____unk

_____ain _____iangle

*Reading words that begin with **tr***

A JUGGLING ACT

_____ab

_____ize

_____ee

_____um

_____ass

Write the missing blend for each word. Use the letters on the stand.

_____uck

_____ick

_____ush

_____ess

_____og

_____apes

br   cr   dr
fr   gr   pr   tr

GRETA'S TRIP

Write the correct word to complete
each sentence.

1. Greta is going on a _____.
    trip, trick

2. She is packing her _____.
    tree, trunk

3. It is big and _____.
    gray, grow

4. Greta will take a _____.
    dry, dress

5. It has _____ flowers.
    price, pretty

6. She will take a _____, too.
    brush, brake

7. Greta will eat some _____ on the way.
    fruit, free

8. Greta will have a _____ time!
    grade, grand

*Review of **r** blends*

WHICH WORD?

Write the correct word to complete each sentence.

1. We can _____ at the park.
   skate, skit

2. I like to _____ down the path.
   skin, skip

3. A _____ is black and white.
   skunk, skim

4. A baby has soft _____.
   skid, skin

5. Flora has a long _____.
   skirt, skate

6. That dog looks _____.
   skinny, skill

7. A plane flew across the _____.
   skim, sky

Reading words that begin with sk

23

WORDS IN SMOKE

Use the **sm** words in the smoke to complete the sentences.

smoke   smell   smock
smile   smooth   small
smashed

1. The boy has a big (**S**) ___ ___ ___ ___ on his face.

2. I wear a ___ ___ ___ ◯ ___ when I paint.

3. The ball ___ ___ ___ ___ ◯ ___ ___ the window.

4. The fire made a lot of ___ ___ ◯ ___ ___ .

5. A baby's skin is ___ ___ ◯ ___ ___ ___ .

6. This cap is too ___ ___ ___ ◯ ___ for me.

7. These cookies ◯ ___ ___ ___ ___ good!

Try this riddle!

Riddle: Why are fish so smart?

To find the answer, print the circled letters in order on the lines.

Answer: They travel in __**S**__ ___ ___ ___ ___ ___ ___ !

Reading words that begin with sm

SNIPPER'S SNAPSHOT

Here's a snapshot of Snipper. Fill in the blanks below to tell about the picture. Use the **sn** words in the box.

snail	snake	snow	sneakers	snacks	snowman

1. Snipper has _____ on his feet.

2. He has a bag of _____ in his hand.

3. A small _____ is sitting on a rock.

4. A long _____ is sliding along the ground.

5. There is _____ on the ground.

6. A _____ stands behind Snipper.

*Reading words that begin with **sn***

A WEB OF WORDS

Add **sp** to the words in the web. Then use the words
to complete the sentences.

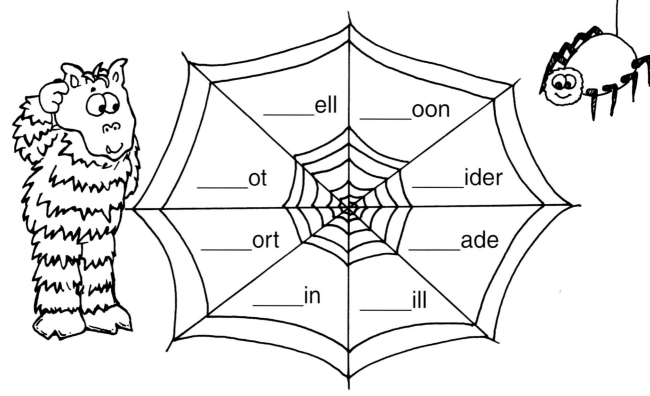

_____ell _____oon

_____ot _____ider

_____ort _____ade

_____in _____ill

1. A _____ has eight legs.

2. Cleo can _____ her top fast.

3. Bruno used a _____ to dig a hole.

4. Crusty can _____ words well.

5. What _____ do you like to play?

6. My dog has a black _____ on his nose.

7. I need a _____ to eat my oatmeal.

8. Try not to _____ the milk.

*Reading words that begin with **sp***

TO THE STORE

Help Stu get to the store. Circle the **st** word for each picture on the path. Then write the words on the lines.

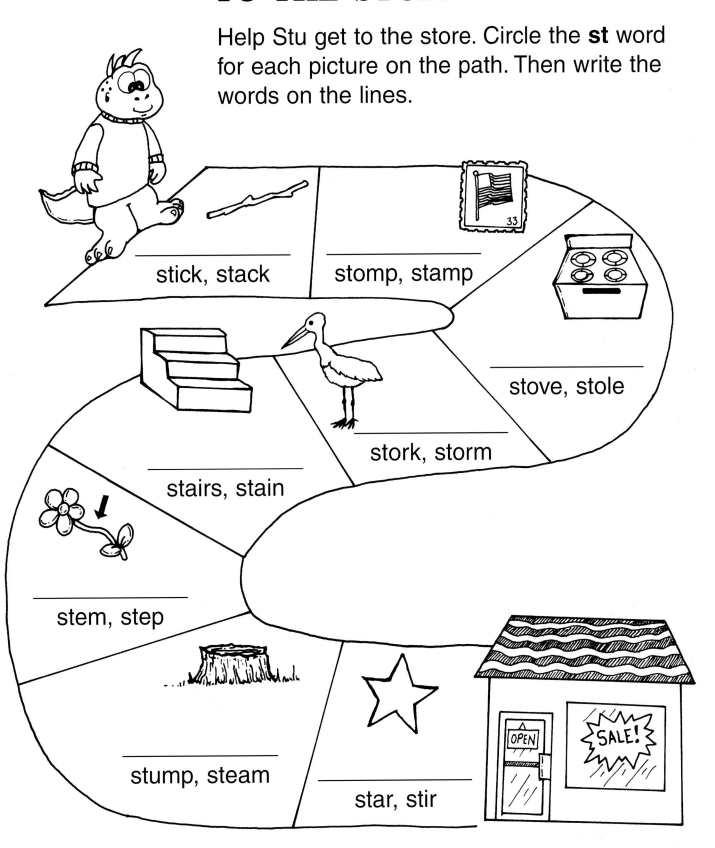

stick, stack

stomp, stamp

stove, stole

stork, storm

stairs, stain

stem, step

stump, steam

star, stir

VACATION FUN

Complete each sentence. Use the **sw** words in the box.

| swim | swing | swimmers | sweet | sweeps |

1. The monsters _____ in the lake.

2. They are good _____.

3. One monster sits on a _____.

4. Another monster _____ with a broom.

5. Later, the monsters will have a _____ treat.

What do you like to do on your vacation?

_____

_____

Reading words that begin with ***sw***

A STONY PATH

Help Stella get to her pet snake. Say the name of each picture on the path. Circle the blend you hear.

sp   st

sm   st

sk   sm

sw   sn

sk   sp

st   sp

sp   sk

sm   sw

sm   sn

sn   sp

sp   st

sn   sk

st   sw

sp   sm

SKIPPY'S FRIENDS

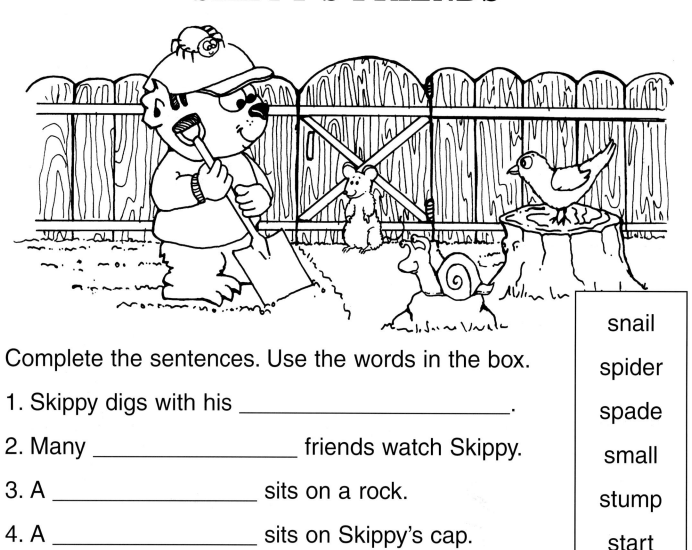

Complete the sentences. Use the words in the box.

1. Skippy digs with his _____.

2. Many _____ friends watch Skippy.

3. A _____ sits on a rock.

4. A _____ sits on Skippy's cap.

5. A mouse _____ by the gate.

6. A bird stands on a _____.

7. Soon Skippy's garden will _____ to grow!

snail

spider

spade

small

stump

start

stands

What would you plant in a garden? Draw a picture to show your answer.

30

Review of s blends

A FUNNY FELLOW

Look at the pictures below. Use the code to color the spaces.

Code

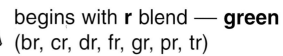

begins with **l** blend — **blue** (bl, cl, fl, gl, pl)

begins with **r** blend — **green** (br, cr, dr, fr, gr, pr, tr)

begins with **s** blend — **brown** (sk, sm, sn, sp, st, sw)

What is in the puzzle? Circle your answer.

bluebird   frog   snake

A FIELD OF FLOWERS

Read the riddles. Write the answers on the matching flowers. Use the words on the sign.

plum	crib	train
flute	frog	swim
grass	snake	spade

1. This animal has no legs.

2. This is a fruit.

3. You can blow in this to make a tune.

4. A baby sleeps in this.

5. This animal can jump.

6. This takes you places.

7. This helps you dig.

8. You do this in the water.

9. This is a green plant.

1 _____

2 _____

3 _____

4 _____

5 _____

6 _____

7 _____

8 _____

9 _____

Reading words that have l, r, or s blends

ON THE GO

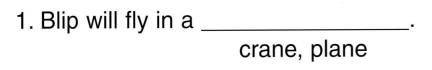

Write the correct word to complete
each sentence.

1. Blip will fly in a _____.
   crane, plane

2. Cleo is going to ride the _____.
   brake, train

3. Slimy will ride in a _____.
   truck, clock

4. Bruno will _____ to the park.
   skate, crate

5. Greta is going on a _____ boat.
   stall, small

6. Dru will ride his bike on the _____.
   trail, snail

7. Glib will go on a car _____.
   trip, slip

Review of l, r, and s blends

CHECK OUT THESE WORDS

Help Chester finish the list. Write **ch** on the lines to complete the words. Then draw a line from each word to its matching picture.

_____ain

_____air

pea_____

_____ick

_____est

mat_____

coa_____

_____erry

Reading words that begin or end with ch

CROSSWORD TIME

Fill in the puzzle with words from the box. Use the picture clues to help you.

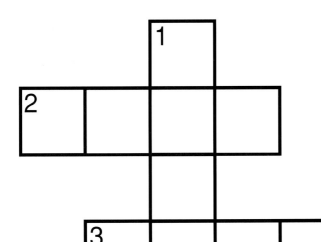

Across

2.

3.

6.

Down

1.

4.

5.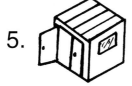

6.

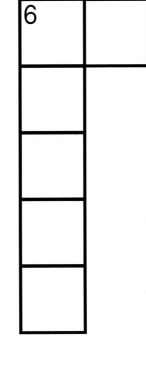

FARM FRIENDS

Help Chester take the chick and the sheep home to the farmer.
Write **ch** or **sh** on the path to make words.

_____ine

_____ain

_____ave

_____ed

_____ake

_____eck

fi_____

pea_____

_____ase

_____est

ri_____

_____ape

tra_____

_____ell

_____art

Review of consonant digraphs ch and sh

THINK, THEO, THINK!

Help Theo figure out the answer to each riddle below. Write the words from the box on the correct lines.

moth	thin	bath	thorn
teeth	thirty	thirsty	thumb

1. This is part of your hand. _____

2. This is a number. _____

3. These help you eat. _____

4. This means **not thick**. _____

5. This is a sharp part of a stem. _____

6. This helps you get clean. _____

7. This is how you may feel when you are hot.

_____

8. This insect looks like a butterfly. _____

WHAT A LOAD!

Add **wh** to complete the words in the wheelbarrow. Then use the words to finish the sentences.

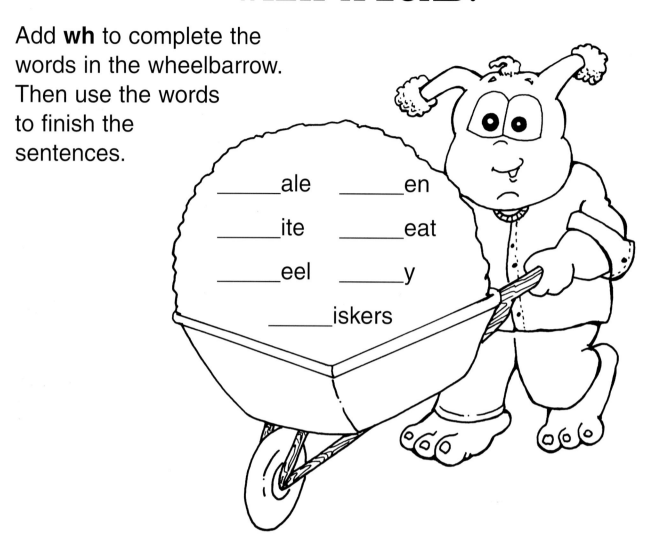

_____ale   _____en

_____ite   _____eat

_____eel   _____y

_____iskers

1. My truck has a broken _____.

2. A _____ is a big animal.

3. I will get milk _____ I go to the store.

4. My uncle grows _____ on his farm.

5. A skunk has _____ stripes.

6. Cats have many _____.

7. I do not know _____ he is not here yet.

*Reading words that begin with **wh***

A WORD MAKER

The monsters have a machine that makes words. But some letters are missing from the words below! Fill in the blanks with **th** or **wh** to complete the words.

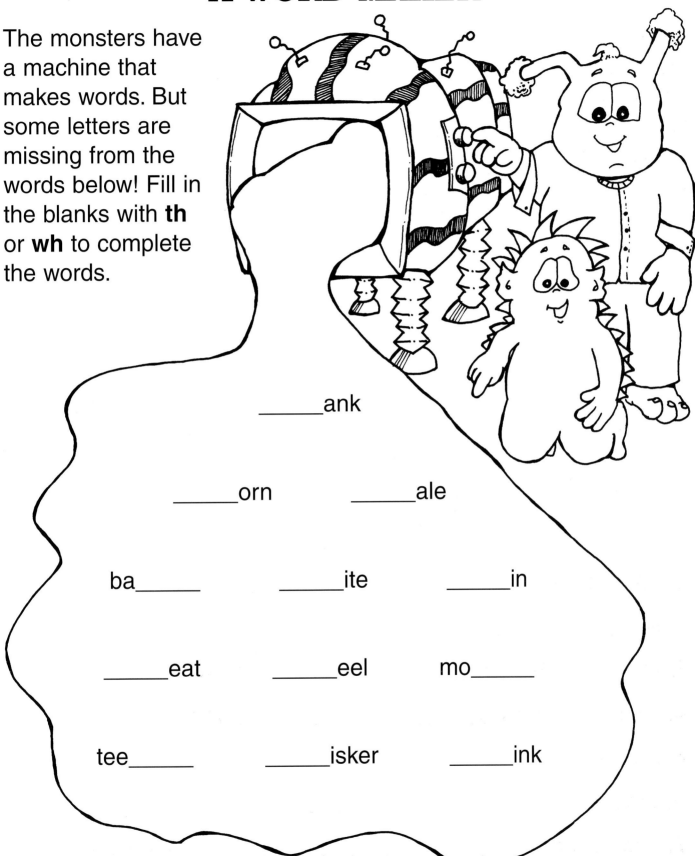

_____ank

_____orn   _____ale

ba_____   _____ite   _____in

_____eat   _____eel   mo_____

tee_____   _____isker   _____ink

WHAT'S ON THE SHELF?

Write **ch, sh, th,** or **wh** on the lines to label the things on each shelf.

_____ip   _____eel   _____ain

_____ick   _____ell   mo_____

_____ale   _____est   di_____

pea_____   _____eep   clo_____

*Review of consonant digraphs **ch, sh, th,** and **wh***

COSTUME FUN

The monsters are dressed up for a costume party! Read about their outfits below. Finish each sentence with the correct word.

1. Blip is dressed as a _____.
   whale, shale

2. Greta is dressed as a _____.
   cheap, sheep

3. Flora has on a long _____.
   sheet, wheat

4. Dru is a big _____.
   peach, teeth

5. Cleo is dressed as a _____.
   thicken, chicken

6. Bruno is dressed as a _____.
   match, moth

7. Glib is a pretty _____.
   shell, chill

*Reading words containing consonant digraphs **ch**, **sh**, **th**, and **wh***

A SLEEPY BUNCH

Look at each picture on the quilt. Say its name. Circle the beginning sound you hear.

Distinguishing consonant blends and digraphs

IN THE KITCHEN

Look at the picture. Find the things listed below and color them.

Color blue.	Color green.	Color yellow.	Color red.
clock	broom	snail	chair
glass	frog	spoon	moth
plate	grapes	stove	shelf

Reading words containing consonant blends and digraphs

TRAVEL GAME

This is a game for two players. Ask a parent or a friend to play with you. You will need one coin and two markers.

Directions

1. Each player places a marker on the space marked **Home**.

2. Take turns flipping the coin and moving your marker along the game board. If the coin lands heads up, move one space. If it lands tails up, move two spaces.

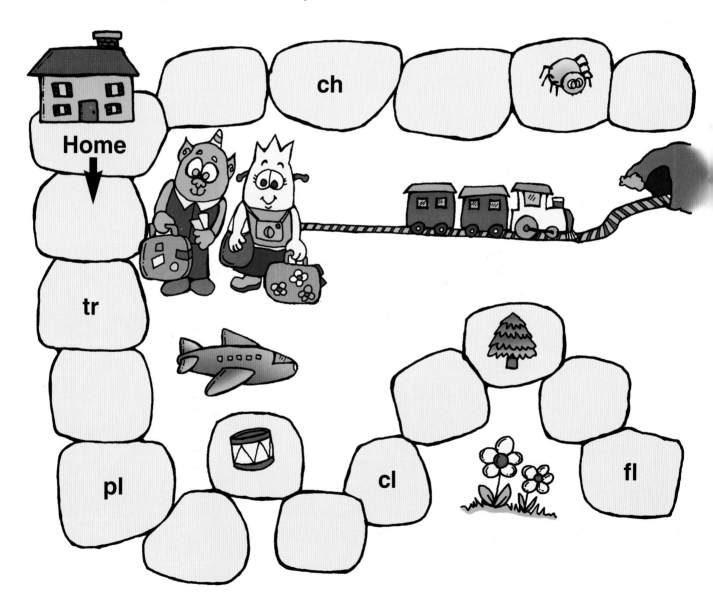

Review of consonant blends and digraphs

3. If a player lands on a letter pair, he or she says a word that begins with that sound and moves an extra space forward.

4. If a player lands on a picture, he or she names it and tells which letter pair makes the beginning sound. Then the player moves an extra space forward.

5. The first player to get back **Home** wins.

Review of consonant blends and digraphs

Answers

Page 6
1. blimp
2. bluebird, blue
3. blanket
4. block

The pictures should be colored as follows: blimp–red; bird–blue; blanket–yellow; block–green.

Page 7
1. clock
2. clam
3. claws
4. clay
5. club

Parent: Child should label the pictures using the five words above.

Page 8
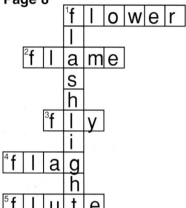

Page 9
1. glad
2. glass
3. glue
4. globe
5. glasses

Answers to question will vary.

Page 10
plant
plate
plane
plug
plum
plank

Page 11
1. sleeping
2. slippers
3. slug
4. sled
5. sliding
6. slick

Page 12
flag **cl**ock **pl**ant
block **sl**ide **sl**ed
clam **gl**obe **fl**ute
plane **bl**anket **gl**ue

Page 13
1. blocks
2. clay
3. flag
4. globe
5. plane
6. slide
7. glue
8. sled

Page 14
bride brick branch
braid brush bracelet

Page 15
The words on the crowns should be completed with the letters **cr**.
1. crab
2. crib
3. cracker
4. croak
5. crayon
6. crack
7. cream

Page 16
The words in the box should be completed with the letters **dr**.
dragon dress drill
drape drum dresser

Page 17
1. frog
2. fruit
3. fry
4. frame
5. free
6. frost
7. fresh

Page 18
1. grass
2. green
3. grin
4. grape
5. grand

Pictures will vary.

Page 19
1. print
2. prize
3. price
4. prick
5. prank
6. pretty
7. problem

Page 20
The words on the truck should be completed with the letters **tr**.
tree
tray
train
triangle
truck
trunk

Page 21

Page 22
1. trip
2. trunk
3. gray
4. dress
5. pretty
6. brush
7. fruit
8. grand

Page 23
1. skate
2. skip
3. skunk
4. skin
5. skirt
6. skinny
7. sky

Page 24
1. smile
2. smock
3. smashed
4. smoke
5. smooth
6. small
7. smell

Answer: They travel in s c h o o l s!

Page 25
1. sneakers
2. snacks
3. snail
4. snake
5. snow
6. snowman

Page 26
The words on the web should be completed with the letters **sp**.
1. spider
2. spin
3. spade
4. spell
5. sport
6. spot
7. spoon
8. spill

Page 27
These words should be circled and written on the lines on the path: stick, stamp, stove, stork, stairs, stem, stump, star.

Page 28
1. swim   4. sweeps
2. swimmers   5. sweet
3. swing
Answers to the question will vary.

Page 29

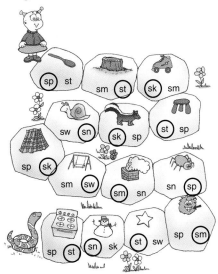

Page 30
1. spade   5. stands
2. small   6. stump
3. snail   7. start
4. spider
Answers and drawings for question will vary.

Page 31
These **l** blend objects should be colored blue: clock, flower, flute, glass, flag, block, plane.
These **r** blend objects should be colored green: crown, drum, tree, grapes, brush, truck.
These **s** blend objects should be colored brown: skate, skirt, spoon, spider, snail, star, snowman.

A frog is in the puzzle.

Page 32
1. snake   6. train
2. plum   7. spade
3. flute   8. swim
4. crib   9. grass
5. frog

Page 33
1. plane   5. small
2. train   6. trail
3. truck   7. trip
4. skate

Page 34
The words in the list should be completed with the letters **ch**.
Parent: Child should draw a line from each word to its matching picture.

Page 35

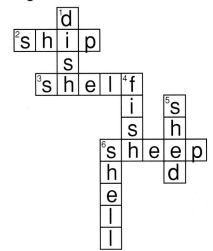

Page 36
These words should be completed on the path: **sh**ine, **ch**ain, **sh**ave, **ch**eck, **sh**ake, **sh**ed, fi**sh**, pea**ch**, **ch**ase, **ch**est, ri**ch**, **sh**ape, tra**sh**, **sh**ell, **ch**art.

Page 37
1. thumb   5. thorn
2. thirty   6. bath
3. teeth   7. thirsty
4. thin   8. moth

Page 38
The words on the wheelbarrow should be completed with the letters **wh**.

1. wheel   5. white
2. whale   6. whiskers
3. when   7. why
4. wheat

Page 39
These words should be completed: **th**ank, **th**orn, **wh**ale, ba**th**, **wh**ite, **th**in, **wh**eat, **wh**eel, mo**th**, tee**th**, **wh**isker, **th**ink.

Page 40
ship   **wh**eel   **ch**ain
chick   **sh**ell   mo**th**
whale   **ch**est   di**sh**
pea**ch**   **sh**eep   clo**th**

Page 41
1. whale   5. chicken
2. sheep   6. moth
3. sheet   7. shell
4. peach

Page 42

Page 43
Parent: Child should color the items in the picture according to the directions.

Pages 44–45
The blends in the names of the pictures on the game board are as follows:
drum – dr   frog – fr
tree – tr   snake – sn
snowman – sn   spider – sp